REAL
SIMPLE
PARENTING

3 Simple Steps to Invest in Your Child's Character Bank

Janis Hanson & Susan vonEhrenkrook

P.S. We are here for you! always! to brain-
storm, vent, talk out loud + talk in the
Being-a-Parent-that-loves-his-boys! ♥

ISBN:1499717377
ISBN-13:9781499717372

We are dedicating this book to you~

the dedicated parent.

CONTENTS

ACKNOWLEDGEMENTS

We are thankful for our husbands letting us retire so we could write this book and speak full time on what we are passionate about.

We are thankful for the children that have passed through our lives onto their own to become the amazing adults they are today.

We are thankful for the grandchildren that we have been blessed with and don't have to correct!

We are thankful for those who helped edit and enhance our book. First, thank you to Amanda von Ehrenkrook for using her time and talents to painstakingly go through every word and punctuation mark. Thank you to our husbands, Dave and Mark and for their wise insight. Thank you to April and Jeremy Lee for adding the entertainment element. And thank you to Heather Hanson for helping design our cover.

And finally, we are thankful that you are reading our book and want to invest in your child's character bank using our three simple steps. What a privilege it is to come along side you!

.

Chapter 1

START

"Before I got married I had six theories about raising
children; now, I have six children
and no theories."
John Wilmot, 2nd Earl of Rochester (1647-1680)

"Mom, what's a condom?" That was the question my (*Janis*) sixth grader asked me the moment he stepped in the house after school one day. Ryan was my first born, so this was definitely new ground for me. The first thing I thought was how grateful I was that he brought the question home instead of asking his friends. The second thing I thought was, *I got this*, after all, I had just spent the year researching and writing curriculum on sexual addiction for a non-profit organization.

I asked Ryan to sit down and after a somewhat lengthy, but age-appropriate and age-sensitive explanation, I asked him if he had any questions about what I just shared. His eyes were as big as saucers and I could barely hear him, when he said, *"I thought they were houses or something."* It would have been a good idea for me to clarify what he was really looking for, the definition of a CONDO, before I went off on my discourse.

We had to clarify before writing this book to determine what parents really wanted as well. We could have gone on and on espousing parenting research and theories, since between us we have over six decades of research and experience. But we know from talking to parents what you are looking for, **REAL** (tried and true), SIMPLE (easy to use) **PARENTING.**

The core of **REAL**SIMPLE**PARENTING** (**RSP**) is just three simple steps:

1. Instruct

2. Reflect

3. Correct

We will help you with how to **Instruct** and follow-through on the values that you believe are important in shaping your child. And because we want you to be a fair and wise parent, we will ask you to **Reflect**; this will give your child the benefit of the doubt. Lastly, we are going to show you how to **Correct** using a caring model. These three little steps are going to make a big difference in your parenting!

Every day you choose to consistently parent with our three simple steps, you are helping your child develop habits that will prepare him or her for both personal and public success. You will be investing in your child's character bank, *ka-ching*! But our primary objective in writing this is not for you to put out the perfect child, but that *you* would not be put out as a parent. And we know what puts you out. It's the constant asking, telling, pleading, begging and battling in any given day and waking up to start it all over again. That all stops now as we make your job easier!

Here are just some of the short and long term benefits you, as a parent, can experience with **RSP**:

❖ You speak just once and your child listens to you and does what you ask.

❖ You have a long and relaxing bath after your three year old gets and stays in bed.

❖ You have a stress free morning while your children get up and get ready for school by themselves.

❖ You experience peace and harmony in your home with siblings resolving their own conflict. (*Uh huh, we got you now!*)

❖ Your teenager looks you in the eyes and treats you with respect.

Granted, we are not saying we saw these dividends every day, but for the most part, this is what we experienced by consistently parenting with **RSP.** And to think, it just takes three steps! Our sincere desire for you is that you see how simple (maybe not always easy) it is to parent using these steps.

We encourage you to stop whenever you see the **"Bring It Home"** symbol and begin using what you learn immediately. As a result of applying what you read and taking this journey with us, we hope you come to love parenting as much as we did. And that you say with conviction, *"Please raise my children for me!"* Just kidding!

Bring it Home

Write down one thing your child is doing that's driving you crazy right now. Or maybe you are reading this to prepare yourself for parenting. In that case, you could write down a possible concern you might have or something you observed from other families. You will be coming back to this at the end of each chapter.

_____

_____

_____

Chapter 2

STYLES

> "Kids, just because I don't care
> doesn't mean I'm not listening."
> Homer Simpson

"Thinking of television mothers, who would you most like to have had as a mom when you were growing up?"

This question was taken as an online survey in 2012, and the top three moms were:

1. June Cleaver of *Leave it to Beaver*. She was a stay at home mom.

2. Clair Huxtable of *The Cosby Show*. She balanced home and career.

3. Carol Brady of *The Brady Bunch*. She parented a blended family.

The Harris Poll® of 2,345 adults surveyed online between April 10 and 15, 2012 by Harris Interactive®.

June Cleaver was number one, and has been number one, since the 1950's when she appeared on TV doing housework in her apron and pearls. You may not be familiar with June Cleaver but we wonder who would you pick to be the ideal mom.

Ward Cleaver: *"What are you looking for?"*
June Cleaver: *"I lost one of my wings."*
(From *Leave it to Beaver*)

Why has June Cleaver remained on top for over 50 years? The best answer is from June Cleaver herself, Barbara Billingsly:

"Some people think she (June Cleaver) was weakish, but I don't. She was the love in that family. I think everybody would like a family like that. Wouldn't it be nice if you came home from school and there was mom standing there with her little apron and cookies waiting?" 1997 *TV Guide*

We're not exactly sure what you are thinking about that comment right now, but we're pretty sure it goes something like this: *"That sounds nice, the little mom in the apron with the warm cookies and all, but who has that kind of time? I'm too busy running the kids all over town, getting them to their activities."* Or, you are working full-time (outside the home), feeling guilty about not being the "ideal parent" and devouring a bag of cookies right now.

June Cleaver has yet to be dethroned because she portrayed what is perceived to be the best parenting style. Not many have come close to her, in fact, today we are inundated with pathetic parenting styles. Right away, Homer Simpson comes to our mind as the worst parenting style EVER!

We have condensed the broad range of parents down to four main parenting styles. Here they are along with their on-screen personification:

1. **Dominant** - "Mother" Gothel from *Tangled*

2. **Detached** - Homer Simpson from *The Simpsons*

3. **Lenient** - Kitty from *That 70's Show*

4. **Loving and Firm** – Huxtables from *The Cosby Show*

You can probably come up with your own TV characters for each style as well.

Let's look further at the traits each style displays in the following chart.

RSP - Four Parenting Styles

Dominant	More Control	Loving & Firm
Rigid Over-ruling Unapproachable High Expectations Committed to Structure		Nurturing Offers Guidance Sets Boundaries Open Communication Committed to Character

Less Caring ———————————————— More Caring

Detached	Less Control	Lenient
Indifferent Distracted Self-absorbed Minimal Interaction Committed to Self		Indulgent Inconsistent Few Boundaries Friend vs. Parent Committed to Happiness

Look again at the last characteristic of each parenting style. Did you notice what each parent is committed to in regards to their child? That commitment determines where the parent will invest their resources.

Now that you have a clear picture of what these four parenting styles look like, let's see what they would typically say as a parent.

Pick the parenting style that you think best represents the comment.

"I am going to count to three."
- ○ Dominant
- ○ Detached
- ○ Lenient
- ○ Loving and Firm

"Get your mother to help you, I'm busy."
- ○ Dominant
- ○ Detached
- ○ Lenient
- ○ Loving and Firm

"I need more information before I can make a decision."
- ○ Dominant
- ○ Detached
- ○ Lenient
- ○ Loving and Firm

"Rules are rules! No child of mine is going to…"
- ○ Dominant
- ○ Detached
- ○ Lenient
- ○ Loving and Firm

Do you want to know if you got them right?
- ❖ Excessive counting, to avoid a confrontation, would be the response of a *lenient* parent.
- ❖ The *detached* parent would have anyone else, but themselves, help their child.
- ❖ It is the *loving and firm* parent that would problem-solve with their child.

❖ And the *dominant* parent would be committed to the rules and not stop to hear the heart of their child.

We want to highlight the loving and firm parent and what their interaction offers their children by looking at a study. The study was looking at the effects of a fence bordering a playground and how it would impact preschoolers. (This study was cited by the American Society of Landscape Architects for the purpose of designing an orphanage in Baldwin County Alabama.) Teachers were asked to take their young students to a fenced playground and then to an unfenced one. They were told to simply observe how the preschoolers played in each area. The teachers noted that in the fenced playground the children freely explored within the boundaries, but in the unfenced area they actually huddled around their teachers.

The results of the study showed that children felt more secure, and were free to develop their sense of self, in a safe environment with limits. In the same way, the loving and firm parent provides their children with the desired boundaries and the freedom to explore. This parenting style offers the child care and control much like the fence on a playground.

Think of your own upbringing now and how you felt as a child growing up. Did you feel secure? How were you parented?

Which of the four parenting styles did your parent(s) demonstrate?

Mother	**Father**
o Dominant	o Dominant
o Detached	o Detached
o Lenient	o Lenient
o Loving and Firm	o Loving and Firm

The style your parent(s) demonstrated is your first point of reference and will influence how you tend to parent. Some experts believe you will parent in the exact opposite way.

What is your parenting style?
- o Dominant
- o Detached
- o Lenient
- o Loving and Firm

To help you define your parenting style, you might want to think through each child, as your parenting style may vary with each one. It might also help to ask your spouse or a good friend for their opinion. I (*Janis*) asked my children, when they were old enough, how they felt I was parenting them. They were brutally honest, with the two older ones, sharing that I was more lenient with my last daughter. I made a concerted effort to be more consistent after that.

As Barbara Billingsly said, most of us wish we had loving and firm parents growing up. And it is that parenting style we all strive for. However, we personally know, making it a goal to be a loving and firm parent could be challenging with potential obstacles such as:

- ❖ Overwhelming fatigue, being the sole parent and provider.

- ❖ Limited availability, with both parents employed outside the home.

- ❖ Distracted, spending time on the internet for work, social media and recreation.

- ❖ A lack of parental knowledge and skills, based on your background.

We want you to know, regardless of what you bring to the parenting table, whatever the obstacle, there is hope. But we also know that what you think you believe, and what you believe you act upon.

Wherever you are in this evolving thought process, we know you will be able to benefit as a parent using the following concept. This concept, *Goal vs. Desire,* is one of our favorite tools in life. It's a basic, easy to use, every day tool much like a hammer and screwdriver. It's from the book, *The Marriage Builder* by Dr. Larry Crabb. (You will be thankful for our simplified version.)

Goal vs. Desire

A *goal* is something you want that does not involve another person or any factor beyond your control. You own it 100%.

A *desire* is something you want that involves factors that are not under your control, such as another person.

It's just that easy, but to help clarify, let's have a little quiz.

Is it a *goal* or *desire* that you get a promotion in your job?
Getting a promotion can only be a *desire* because it involves your boss. The *goal* is to be the best employee you know how to be. And when you feel it is the right time, you can ask for the promotion.

Is it a *goal* or a *desire* that you lose weight?
This is a *goal,* you own it 100%. I know you want to say to your husband, *"You made me eat that Blizzard®!"* but he does not put food in your mouth. This truth is both freeing and empowering; no one, but yourself, can prevent you from reaching your healthy weight.

Is it a *goal* or a *desire* that you have well behaved children?

It's a fantasy! ☺ While it is an immense *desire* that your children behave and turn out to be amazing adults, you cannot make this a *goal*. The *goal* is to be the best parent you know how to be. This truth can be freeing as well. You don't own how your children turn out and that has got to take an enormous amount of weight off your heart and shoulders.

Isn't that a great tool or concept? Despite all your hang ups, dysfunctional background, obstacles, etc., you can be a loving and firm parent. You own it 100%! This tool can change your thinking for good!

I can remember vividly the day I *(Janis)* decided to make it a *goal* to be a loving and firm parent. Given my background, it was not easy. I have somewhat of a *Cinderella* story. My mother died when I was just months old and that drastically changed the dynamics of our family. My dad was a detached father with four little girls under the age of six. He married, what I perceived to be, the dominant wicked stepmother who brought two sons of her own. They went on to have two more children and, in short order, we became a dysfunctional family of 10! I cannot remember a single moment of tender physical contact from either parent. Which parenting style do you think I started off as? My natural inclination was to love my child but to NOT be firm. In the absence of knowing what to do, I did nothing and became a lenient parent. I could hear Dr. Phil say, *"And how's that working for you?"*

My first born son, Ryan, quickly became an out of control toddler. I can remember him throwing screaming fits in Target (yes, I was that mom), emptying kitchen cabinets at friends' homes and refusing to take my hand crossing busy streets.

I finally conceded, I didn't have a clue how to parent. My husband and I humbled ourselves and asked a wonderful couple with four amazing teens to mentor us. And thus began my quest to become a loving and firm parent.

Our *desire* is that your *goal* as a loving and firm parent begins here, or continues to be nurtured here. RSP will help you establish an environment in which your child is free to grow and explore with a sense of safety, peace and predictability. We want to help you erect the "fence" of care and control for your child, in order for them to have the greatest possible chance of becoming a secure adult.

A true life account of this is Ben Carson who was raised by a single mother, living in Chicago in the 1960's, with just a third grade education. Her boys thrived with her loving and firm boundaries in which she created a home that was conducive to learning and growth. Ben Carson went on to be an internationally acclaimed brain surgeon and his brother a rocket scientist.

OK, so maybe we can't all raise surgeons and scientists, but we can, despite our obstacles, be loving and firm parents.

 Bring it Home

In chapter one we asked you to write down something that is driving you crazy. What do you *think* a loving and firm parent would do? In your home this week listen to how you talk. Do you sound like a loving and firm parent?

Chapter 3

INVEST

"Some people treat life like a slot machine,
trying to put in as little as possible and hoping to hit a
jackpot. Wiser people think of life as a solid investment from
which they receive in terms of what they put in."
Roger Hull, Reader's Digest

There is a big difference between the parenting styles of June Cleaver and Homer Simpson and the investments they made in the lives of their children. On TV, June Cleaver was a stay at home mom but in real life, the actress, Barbara Billingsly worked outside the home. She portrayed on *Leave it to Beaver* the mom she was in reality. She focused on what was truly important, taking time to build meaningful relationships.

When my (*Janis*) kids were small I had a home business, so I had the luxury of being there when the kids came home from school. And, yes, minus the apron and pearls, on most days I had a special snack waiting for them. The snack was the incentive to stop and sit with me. I learned that if they were going to share what mattered most in their day it was then. I geared the conversation around the *unstructured* part of their day, such as recess and relationships, to invest in their character.

- ❖ Who did you sit with on the bus?

- ❖ Who did you play with at recess and what did you do?

- ❖ How will you know if that person is going to be a good friend?

- ❖ What did you do that was kind today?

You need to take the time to stop and hear the heart of your child and stay as connected as possible. The door to intimacy that is opened from establishing trust while they are young is more likely to remain unlocked as they grow into adolescents and teens. We realize there are so many *good* activities to involve your children in, but don't lose focus on what is truly important. Do not let the good become the enemy of the very best! No one is more significant than you in shaping and molding your child's character.

And when it comes to character, we know children are born with a zero balance! Character is the moral, ethical qualities that make up an individual. As parents, we need to be committed to invest in this area. All too often, parents will make intentional, consistent deposits to their child's college fund but invest very little in their child's character bank.

Children are predisposed to grabbing toys, pushing to be first in line and screaming when they want something. Have you ever had to teach your child to be greedy or to stop sharing too much? Did you have to give them a heads up about lying in order to cover their tracks? Of course not! They come out of the crib saying, '*MINE!*' and '*ME*'. Left to their own, children are basically selfish.

Have you ever seriously and specifically thought about what qualities or values you would like to invest in your child? Remember, it doesn't happen by accident and it's never too early to start.

Look at the following list of qualities or values you could invest in your child's character bank. Try to pick your top 12 values to give you the advantage in the game of parenting. (*Like the Seattle Seahawks have their "12th Man" to give them the advantage— being from Washington, we couldn't resist.*)

Acceptance	Friendship	Loyalty
Beauty	Forgiveness	Maturity
Communication	Generosity	Patience
Community	Grace	Perseverance
Compassion	Gratitude	Respect
Consistency	Health	Responsibility
Courage	Honesty	Security
Creativity	Hope	Self-discipline
Decisiveness	Humility	Sharing
Education	Humor	Trustworthiness
Enthusiasm	Integrity	_____
Excellence	Justice	_____
Faith	Kindness	_____
Family	Love	_____

If you are married, you could also have your spouse pick their 12. And then, mutually agree on the 12 values that you will instill in your family.

In my (*Susan*) early parenting years, I heard a renown pediatric psychologist, Dr. James Dobson, speak on parenting. He shared his list of 70 values that he used with his own children. After listening to Dr. Dobson, my husband, Mark, and I started off gung-ho. We initially chose 40 values we wanted to invest in our children, but it soon became clear what an unrealistic and overwhelming goal we had set for ourselves. We distilled our list of 40 down to 12, and then narrowed it down further to our *super six*. We were committed to love, laughter, integrity, faith, forgiveness and encouragement. (You can see I added some that were not on the list. Feel free to do the same.)

We lived out these values in our every-day, ordinary lives and reinforced them with our children. So much so, that I can remember my 16 year-old son throwing up his hands in the car asking, *"Does everything have to be a teachable moment?"* Now, I am watching my son use his own teachable moments with the hundreds of teens he leads as he invests in their character.

The list of qualities and values we provided is certainly not an exhaustive one, but it's a good place to start. You will need to do a thorough job of teaching these values to your child. Remember, they are not born with these qualities, nor are they instinctive by nature. Begin now distilling your list of 12 down to your *super six*.

Next, let us give you 6 qualities and how you could teach them to your child. You cannot role-model or role-play them too much.

1. **Sharing**

   Sit down with a *new* toy between you and your child. You play with the toy first. Be animated so as to keep the child's attention. The desired behavior while you play with the toy is for your child to patiently wait. You may need to instruct your child that this is the appropriate and expected behavior while waiting. (Don't worry, we're going to help you with this when we share our three simple steps.) After a few minutes, give the toy to your child and say, *"Your turn now! I'm sharing."*

After he or she plays with the toy for a few minutes say, *"My turn please."* You can elaborate if you see your child hesitate, which is their natural bent. *"Please share with me and I will give the toy right back after I play with it. But if you do not share, I will have to put it away."* If your child does not give the toy back quickly, put it out of sight.

Come back the next day and do it all over again. Once you see you child understands the concept of sharing and waiting nicely, praise the child and give the toy as a reward for sharing.

2. Honesty

Here's a simple activity you can do to teach your child the difference between a truth and a lie. Sit down at the table with your child and place five pennies (or M&M's) in front of them asking, *"How many pennies are there?"*

"One, two, three, four, five." the child counts.

"That is true; I have five pennies." Take away two pennies and say again, *"I have five pennies."*

"Noooo!" the child argues, *"You have three pennies!"*

"That is the truth. I have three pennies. Saying I have five pennies would be a lie. I ALWAYS want you to tell the truth. And I will ALWAYS correct you for lying."

Place the pennies before the child and have them practice "truth" and "lie" as many times as it takes for the child to learn the desired character trait of honesty. After your teaching time, put the pennies in the child's piggy bank (*you eat the M&M's, kidding!*).

3. Communication

"We are going to play a game!" (Games are a great go-to motivational tool.) Using a ball, explain, *"In this game you do <u>not</u> want to be holding the ball. You can only toss the ball to someone when you ask them a question that cannot be answered with a, 'Yes,' or, 'No.' For example, 'What did you do at recess?' would be a good question and you get to toss the ball. 'Did you go out to recess today?' would not be good because they could answer, 'Yes,' or, 'No,' and the ball could not be tossed. I am holding the ball, so I will ask the first question."*

Ask the first open-ended question and toss the ball to the person who answers. That person gets to ask the next question and toss the ball, and so on. The value of listening and communicating is not caught; it's taught! (*Pun intended.*)

To reinforce good communication, when you have guests over for dinner, you could sit with your children before the guests arrive and help them write open-ended questions. They will be more engaged in the conversation, waiting for the guests to answer their own question. This teaches children to not only be good communicators but good listeners as well.

4. Forgiveness

I (*Janis*) also taught forgiveness as one of my *super six*. When the children were very young, my husband, Dave, and I illustrated how unresolved conflict, or being unforgiving can separate us from each other. I realize that this is a complicated concept to teach, but we used something simple to illustrate it. We built a wall using blocks that separated 'action figures' on each side. The action figures represented the children. Each block represented built up feelings of resentment or bitterness that were unresolved or unforgiven. We gave them examples as we built the wall: *"This block is a time when you pinched your sister. This block is for when you hit your brother...Can you think of any other things that could be hurtful to someone? Look how the wall gets higher and higher when you do unkind things."*

Then we asked the children what needs to happen for the 'action figures' to not be separated? The children agreed that the wall needed to be torn down. We explained that the blocks could only be removed by asking for forgiveness when they were in the wrong. As parents, we encouraged them to avoid building walls by treating each other with kindness. Occasionally, I would need to remind them that, *"We don't want even ONE block standing between any of us!"*

This didn't mean that our children were void of conflict, but rather, they knew how to resolve conflict on their own and be forgiving. Now that our adult children are married, we often hear how thankful their spouses are for this character trait we instilled. Also, my favorite byproduct of this is the strong and loving relationships all five of our children have with each other.

5. Acceptance

To teach acceptance, open-mindedness or tolerance of what other people feel and their point of view I (*Susan*) made a simple tool using a Ping-Pong ball. One half of the ball was colored black with a permanent marker, leaving the other half white. The objective was for the child to see the two very different perspectives. I would hold the ball showing just one color and ask, *"What color do you see?"* The child would answer *"White."* *"Are you sure?"* They adamantly would say, *"Yes!"* *"Come and stand over here."* From this new point of view they could see the other half of the ball. *"Now what color is the ball? Yes, it is black. But you said over here it was white? What changed your mind? You have a more complete picture seeing the ball from both sides. It's important before you make up your mind that you try and see the complete picture."*

I started using the ping pong ball as a teaching tool when my kids were about third grade, and have even used it to help resolve marital conflicts in counseling. This is still a great visual reminder in our home today.

6. Love

One of the ways I (*Susan*) helped our children understand how to give and receive love was to teach them about the five love languages from Gary Chapman's book, *The Five Love Languages*. My daughter's love language was physical touch and she demonstrated that by lavishing hugs on everyone! One of her brothers, however, did not receive that well. Since we wanted our children to know and demonstrate each other's love language, we had our son give his sister at least one brief hug a day. She had to learn and appreciate her brother's love language, which was gifts. Rather than constant hugs, she would make him cookies. The lasting impact from teaching this value was watching our adult children give and receive love in their spouse's love language.

We hope these examples get you excited to begin teaching your *super six*. Just imagine the inheritance you will be giving your child! For the rest of their lives, they will be able to withdraw from the overflowing character bank you invested in when they were young.

Remember, although you *desire* that your child embrace these values, your *goal* is to be faithful to teach and live them out each day. You are vital in your child's life and you have limited time. So, let's start investing!

> *"Our children are not our prized possession to do with what we want, but are simply passing through our lives on to theirs."*
> *Howard Hendricks*

 Bring it Home

You wrote down what is driving you crazy in chapter one. Is it related to one of the values on the list? For example, if your child is constantly whining, you may need to teach patience. Can you think of a creative way to teach the value of patience? We would love to hear any of your ideas in teaching values to your child. It would be helpful, with your permission of course, to post them on our website to help other parents: www.realsimpleparenting.com. We are so proud of you for making this investment of time to instill your *super six*.

Chapter 4

INSTRUCT

"The most important step in building character is to establish reasonable expectations and boundaries in advance. Children should know what is and is not acceptable behavior before they are held responsible for those rules. This precondition will eliminate the overwhelming sense of injustice that children feel when they are punished for their accidents, mistakes and blunders. If you haven't defined it...don't enforce it!"
Dr. Dobson

On YouTube there is a video called, *Spoiled Kids in Walmart.* It's been seen over two million times. We are sharing part of it with you to show what NOT to do when it comes to instructing a child!

Dad says, *"Sweetie, we're not getting a toy right now. Put that down. OK? Put that down. Let's get ready to go bye-bye."*

His daughter appears to be about 5 years old and screams, *"Nooo, I need a toy."*

"Do you need a toy? Really? Put that down."

"But I need this toy."

"I know, but gram-mama is going to get you a toy later. Let's put that down. OK?"

She whines and says, *"I waaaaant it."*

"Oh my goodness. Let's put that down now."

This is just 30 seconds into the video and it goes on with more of the same. We counted, he instructs the child to, *"Put that down,"* at least 10 times. Finally, the little girl dissolves into tears and the dad promises her a toy for Christmas!

How many times do you instruct your child? ONCE!

This chapter is going to make the biggest difference in your life as a parent and you are going to love us for it. Think how differently that scene at Walmart could have played out had the dad given good instructions in the car *before* going into the store. Better yet, if he was consistent at home, the little girl would have known he means what he says when he says it.

There are two reasons why you stop and **Instruct**:

1. Establish desired character and behavior.

2. Extinguish undesired character and behavior.

If you use your time and energy in *establishing* what is desirable in your child, you will minimize the time spent *extinguishing* the undesirable. Remember, our main objective is that *you* are not put out as a parent. To accomplish this objective, we want the majority of your time invested in establishing desired character and behavior by giving good instructions. To help you remember this step, instruct, we have broken it down into five C's:

Instruct

1. Choose

2. Calculate

3. Connect

4. Communicate

5. Clarify

You will **Choose** and **Calculate** before you **Connect** with your child. Then, **Communicate** and **Clarify**.

1. Choose

❖ **Sensitivity**
Choose to be sensitive to your child. You may need to limit or eliminate instructions in certain instances such as illness, fatigue or a change in schedule.

❖ **Age-appropriate**
Choose age-appropriate instructions. How will you know if your two year old is capable of mowing the lawn? Ok, that one is obvious. But when it's not, you can network with other parents or check out the infinite resources online. The youngest age most children can understand and follow simple instructions is around 15 months.

Also, whenever possible, give your child the opportunity to be a part of the decision making process. This does two things, first it teaches your child quick decision-making skills that will serve him or her as an adult. Second, and better still, your child will be more motivated thinking it was their idea. An example of this was wanting our daughters to wear a dress for a specific occasion. It was easier to give them three dresses from which they could pick. This moved us beyond the argument of, *"Do I have to wear a dress?"*

❖ **Battles**
Choose your battles wisely! A familiar phrase but worth repeating. How will you know which battles to choose? Ask yourself the following question, *"If I let this go, what could be the long-term consequences?"* This will help you discern between the little infractions, such as mood swings, childish play, etc., and the ones you will need to

follow-through with. (*We are going to help you with this again at the end of the chapter.*)

> **"Hardness of your child's heart is always a battle that you cannot ignore. Do not be overly focused on the details of a given infraction; rather, focus on your child's heart."**
> **USS Parenting**

We speak to parents often and one of the most difficult tasks they share with us is having their child get and stay in bed. We are going to use this example to help illustrate how to apply the five C's. To be consistent with our C's, let's call the little boy, Connor. *Plus, that's the name of my (Janis) only grandson out of eight grandchildren.*

Let's say Connor is three and you know he's capable of staying in bed. You **choose** to instruct Connor to get and stay in bed. You are *sensitive* to his needs and have *age appropriate* expectations—get a drink, go potty, get in bed, read a book and lights out. This is a reasonable routine. But Connor begins to push your limits. He asks for more drinks, goes potty again, wants another book. He holds you captive by pleading for more hugs. Connor is smart and figures out all the angles to gain control. He becomes the master of manipulation. How important is this *battle?*

"If I let this go, what could be the long-term consequences?"

At home, he continues to manipulate you, not eating what is served and asking for special food.

At play-time, he manipulates his friends to play his game his way or he won't play.
At school, he justifies why he doesn't do his homework or is late for class.

38

At work, he cheats on his time card, or, files a false tax return.

I realize that pushing the limits appears innocent at first, but your child's character is involved here. What quality could you be investing in your child's character bank here? In this case, you are instilling respect for authority. Connor needs to know he does not control his world but instead, defers to the authority over him. You are making an investment in his character by choosing to win this battle.

2. Calculate

Before you give instructions, you will have to think through two very important things:

❖ **What will my child gain?**

❖ **What will my child lose?**

When you give instructions, even a young child will weigh their options. They are thinking, *"What will I gain if I obey? What will I lose if I don't?"* As a parent, you will need to have those questions answered, in your own mind, before you instruct your child.

Let's calculate what Connor may gain and lose in the example of getting and staying in bed.

Connor could pick a special snack for the next day and place it on the counter before getting into bed. He will *gain* the snack when he stays in bed. He will *lose* the snack if he gets out of bed.

Connor may have a favorite stuffed animal or a blanket to sleep with. He could *gain* either one of those when he stays in bed or *lose* them when he gets out.

Connor may test your resolve by getting out of bed. But if you follow-through immediately with *gain/lose*, he is more likely to NOT do it again. And if he does, you "up the ante," so to speak. (*We will discuss this at great length in the Correct chapter.*) One more thing, be absolutely certain you can follow-through with what you calculate they will *gain/lose*.

3. Connect

Every time you instruct, get down at your child's level, making eye contact before you speak.

❖ **Eye-Level**

❖ **Eye-Contact**

You are now face to face with your child, making eye contact with each other, *"Connor, look at me."* This shows that you mean business and encourages the child to focus on you. Making eye-contact may need to be your very first instruction.

"Eye-contact"
You could reinforce this skill by playing the following game (Remember, games are a motivational tool that makes learning fun for the child and makes your job easier). Sit across the table from your child and instruct them to look at your eyes. As long as your child maintains eye contact, you give them an M&M every 30 seconds or so. If they break eye contact that ends the game.

"Sweetheart, let's play a game. I have four M&M's. What color are they? Keep looking at my eyes while I talk and you will get all four! Here is your first one. Keep looking. Wow! Good job, the next color is yellow..."

You may need to play this game a few times to teach the desired behavior. You will thank us, in the not so distant future, when your teenager makes eye contact with you and other adults. It is a much needed skill as they go out into the world.

After you connect with your child, at eye-level and with eye-contact, you know you have your child's attention. You are now ready to verbally communicate.

4. Communicate

* ❖ **Speak with a kind but firm voice.**

* ❖ **Be positive.**
  Children respond better to positive instruction. For example you would say to Connor, *"Stay in bed,"* rather than, *"Don't get out of bed!"*

* ❖ ***"Talk less; say more." Swedish Proverb***
  You want to be heard and not have your child tune you out. You are giving clear and concise instructions, not a discourse on your parenting philosophy.

* ❖ **Speak ONCE!**
  Communicate one time and follow-through every time. From here on out, you mean what you say when you say it, and you will follow-though every time! Did we mention that you need to follow-

through? ☺ When your child understands this...life is good!

Let's go back to the example of Connor getting and staying in bed. You **chose** this battle to instill respect for authority. Not to mention, it's important for your child's overall health and your sanity! You **calculated** what he will *gain/lose*. Now you **communicate** your instructions:

> *"Connor, look at me. It's time to go to bed. Let's go potty and pick a special snack for tomorrow. It will be right here on the counter for you to have tomorrow when you stay in bed. Yum! I love what you picked."*

5. Clarify

There are a couple of excellent ways to be absolutely certain your child understands your instructions.

> ❖ **Role-Play**
> Don't assume your child knows what you mean by your instructions. In fact, you can pretty much expect the exact opposite. You need to make it crystal clear and clarify what it will look like when your instructions are followed. One of the best ways to clarify your instructions is to role-play the desired character or behavior. (*You cannot role-play too much. We will be giving you examples of this on the following pages.*)

> ❖ **Have the child repeat back the instructions.**
> In addition to role-playing, clarify your instructions by always having the child repeat them back to you.

> *"What did you hear me say?"*

"Connor, tell me what you will do when I say these three words, 'Go to bed.' Yes, you run like Superman. What will you get if you stay in bed like glue? Yes, the special snack on the counter."

As our children matured, we even had written contracts for dating, times to be home, etc. That way, there was never the argument with our teenager, *"You never said..."* We encourage you to continue having your children repeat back what they heard you say until they move out!

In addition to having Connor repeat back your instructions, you can role-play what *"Go to bed and stay in bed,"* looks like when it's <u>not</u> time for bed.

Role-Play: *"Go To Bed"*
"Connor, we are going to play a game. I want you to sit on the couch like a statue. When I say, 'Go to bed,' you run and get in bed like Superman. And I want you to stay in bed like you are stuck like glue. Ok, wait for the three words...wait...'go to bed!' That was sooo fast like Superman. I cannot even get you out of bed because you are stuck like glue to the sheets! Wow! Let's do it again. 'Go to bed!' Tonight, when I say those three words, I will be excited to see you be superman and stick like glue."

Every child wants to play out his super-hero. You can also link the behavior with the desired value (*super six*) you wish to teach and make a deposit in your child's character bank. *"Connor, you did that EXCELLENT! Everything we do should be done with excellence."*

So often parents flippantly give instructions, assuming their child knows what they mean. A good example of this is when a parent says, *"Clean up."* The child takes their time, does a half-hearted job or simply meanders off and does nothing. The parent quickly becomes frustrated, *"I told you to clean up! Now get over here right now!"* But what do those words, *clean up,* really mean to a child? You would be wise to start with a clean slate and take the time to role-play the desired behavior.

Role-Play: *"Clean Up"*

"Let's play with your blocks together!" After playing with your child say, *"We are going to play a game. When I say the words, 'Please, clean up,' quickly put all the blocks back into the bin and put the bin back where it came from. What are the words I will say? Tell me what you will do when I say, 'Please, clean up.' I am going to go way over to the other side of the room. Wait for those words...'Please clean-up!' Wow, look how fast you are going! Do I see any blocks around? Is the bin back where it belongs? Good job!"*

When you set it up as a game, the child is literally motivated by 'winning or losing' the game. And they gain your praise with a job well done. Don't underestimate a parent's praise. Later, when you ask your child to *"please, clean up"* and they defiantly say no or walk away, you know your instructions were understood and you can move swiftly to correction (our third step).

Role-Play: *"Time to Leave"*

I *(Janis)* can remember, as a young mother, trying to leave the house with all five children. If I had to beg, chase, scream and count to ten in order to get my kids in the car, every time I had to leave the house, I would be spent before I even left the driveway. Instead, I role played the words, *"time to leave,"* when

I did <u>not</u> have to go anywhere. The game was to see how quickly we could put on our shoes and coats, climb into the car seats and buckle up when I said the words, *"time to leave."* After role-playing the expected behavior a number of times, they knew exactly what I meant when I said it was time to go.

I remember family and friends marveling at how easy it was for us to manage all five kids. Although, I thanked them for the compliment, I was thinking to myself, it was definitely NOT easy and could not have happened without good instruction.

We thought you might like a couple more examples in giving instructions, using all 5 C's:

Ryan's Rule of Roaming
I (*Janis*) was renting a home where the yard was in the front of the house. For safety, it was not a great situation. I wanted Ryan to have the freedom to play outside but to not go on the sidewalk or street.

"Ryan, honey, let's bring some toys out to the yard. Wow, they are going to be so fun to play with. Ryan, look at me. Every place that has grass you can play. Follow me...does the sidewalk over here have grass? Does the street have grass? Do you play on those? No. Tell me where you can play with your toys? If you step on the sidewalk or any place that does not have grass I will bring you and your toys in the house. Tell me what will happen if you step off the grass onto the sidewalk or street. I will always be out here with you, and we are going to have sooo much fun!"

And we did have fun because I was not constantly shouting for Ryan to get back on the grass. *Did you see all 5 C's in my instructions?*

How Clean is Clean?

A few times a year I *(Janis)* wanted the children to clean their rooms thoroughly. Not assuming they knew what this meant, I had the older children create a list of things they thought they should do, and helped the younger children write their list. Having them write their own list helped with 'buy in.' I praised them for their ideas and added a few of my own. I helped the younger children clean their rooms but to motivate the older children to work independently I said, *"In an hour I am going to come in your room. I will go over the list with you and if everything is done, I will give you $2.00!"* (That was a lot back then.) *"For every item not completed on the list I will take a quarter away, and you will not be paid until it is done according to what we agreed."* With the instructions in writing and agreed upon, I knew they understood. What will they *gain/lose?* Of course they gain and lose the monetary reward. They also gain my praise and a clean room which they love to play in. Peer pressure helps here too. After the hour was up it was interesting to hear the dialogue between them; about how much each got paid, and what they would do differently the next time. In the future, I simply said, *"Let's get the lists and do a good cleaning,"* and they were off and running. No begging, screaming, counting, etc. How nice is that!

Remember, we said there are two reasons why you stop and **Instruct**:

- ❖ Establish desired character and behavior.

- ❖ Extinguish undesired character and behavior.

Desired	Undesired
Obedience	Disobedience
Responsibility	Irresponsibility
Respect	Disrespect
Values/Ethics	Delinquency

All children exhibit undesirable character and behavior. It is true, that with good instruction you will make a big dent in this. But it's important to recognize and extinguish the undesirable character and behavior *before* there are any long-term consequences.

Disobedience is easy to recognize, it's simply the failure to follow instructions. Most parents are quick to act on disobedience because it's black and white.

Irresponsibility ranges from childish immaturity to being unreliable, inconsistent and blaming others.

Disrespect, such as rolling of the eyes, stomping the feet or not making eye contact, can slip under a parent's radar. Disrespect has the potential to be the most destructive in the long run.

Delinquency is being opposed to the values being taught. It can be observed as wrongful, illegal, or antisocial behavior.

Your initial interaction with your child directly influences the interaction they will have with others. Ignoring an undesirable character or behavior, that may seem insignificant at the time, is like a rock thrown into a pond, which can have a ripple effect over time. This far-reaching impact is what we refer to as the *ripple effect*.

" Ripple Effect"
For example, if you allow your child to be disrespectful to you, by stomping their feet, this child could go on to be rude to a sibling, talk back to a teacher, disregard the law or walk away from unresolved conflict as an adult.

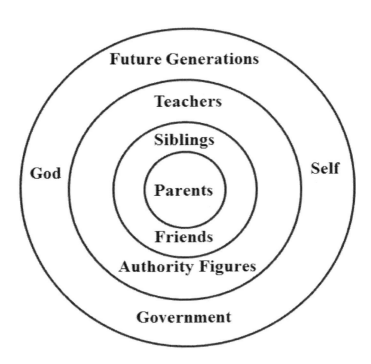

Desired and undesired character and behavior can start and stop with you, the parent. The easiest way to stop the negative *ripple effect*, and to have a positive one instead, is to instruct for the desirable character and behavior when the child is in the womb. ☺

We realize that this first step, instruct, is going to require the greatest commitment from you, the loving and firm parent. It's going to take practice and perhaps brainstorming with other committed parents. *Don't forget you can talk to us on our website, too.*

You may need to overcome some bad habits that are already set in place. It is going to be challenging both mentally and physically. But when you speak one time and your child listens and does what you ask when you ask, you will be thanking us! No more pleading, counting or screaming. AND no more scenes at Walmart!

Bring it Home

Using the 5 C's, write instructions for what is driving you crazy. Here they are again:

- ❖ **Choose** your battles wisely.

- ❖ **Calculate** what your child will *gain/lose.*

- ❖ **Connect** at your child's eye-level; making eye-contact.

- ❖ **Communicate** ONCE!

- ❖ **Clarify** by role-playing and having your child repeat back what you said.

Try and keep your calendar as clear as possible this week so that you can continue to give good instructions and follow-through on every word you say. This is going to make your job as a parent a whole lot easier!!!

Chapter 5

REFLECT

"Be absolutely sure that your children are capable of delivering what you require. Impossible demands put children in an unresolvable conflict.
There is no way out."
James Dobson

This chapter is so short, you'll miss it if you blink twice. Taking a moment to **Reflect** after you instruct does not take long. The reason we have you take this second step is for you to pause and reflect. We want you to *respond* to your child rather than *react*. And it's important to give your child the benefit of the doubt before moving onto the third step, correct. Here are just a few questions to think about:

1. **Am I certain?**
   You need to be absolutely certain your child heard and understood the instructions before moving on to correction. If you gave complete instructions using the 5 C's then you can immediately say, *"Yep, I'm certain!"*

2. **Am I capable?**
   Our goal is to be loving and firm parents, not irrational ones. We need to be capable of following through with what we say. You mean every word you say, when you say it. Because of this, be slow to speak and think it all through before you speak a word to your child. For instance, telling a child he cannot play video games for a week, *(gain/lose)*, may be difficult to follow-through with and may add more stress to the situation.

If you have spoken too soon, and realize you have given your child impossible demands, it's time to humble yourself and say, *"I spoke too soon, let me think about this."* They will have greater trust and respect for you as a parent when you make it right.

3. Am I consistent?

If you have been flippantly telling your child what to do and rarely following through with anything (Walmart dad, we are talking to you), then you can hardly correct your child. With erratic correction comes a sense of injustice on behalf of the child. You could simply say, *"I have been letting this go, but I am on it now."*

I (*Janis*) can remember our oldest daughter treating her siblings with disrespect, which was very out of character for her. She was answering them with curt and rude remarks. I was intent on correcting her until I stopped and listened and heard my own voice mirrored back. I came to the realization that I had been short-tempered that week. Rather than correct her, I had to go back to all the children and ask for forgiveness for my attitude.

> *"Model the rules; teach the rules;*
> *enforce the rules."*
> **Ron Rose**

This is not an exhaustive list of possible questions to ask as you reflect on the situation, but it's a good start. Think about the good instructions you gave to Connor regarding staying in bed. If Connor gets out of bed, you simply take a moment to reflect on the questions. Once you conclude that you are **certain** Connor understands the instructions, and you are **capable** of following through, and you have been **consistent**,

you can move on with certainty, conviction and courage to our third step, correct. (*Is that enough C's for you?*)

Bring it Home

In the last chapter we asked you to give instructions for what is driving you crazy. Take time now to **Reflect.**

❖ Were you *certain* you were heard and understood?

❖ Were you *capable* of following through with *gain/lose*?

❖ Are you being *consistent* in word and action?

Keep it up! ♥

Chapter 6

CORRECT

"Every Year that passes should bring fewer rules, less direct discipline and
more independence for the child."
James Dobson

You are no longer throwing out orders and threats willy-nilly. You are giving good instructions, and with good instructions you seldom need to **Correct.**

So when do you correct? Let's go back to the scenario of Connor getting and staying in bed that we used in the Instruct chapter. Let's recap using the 5 C's:

1. You **chose** to work on this behavior and are certain he's at the right age to get and stay in bed.

2. You **calculated** the cost (*gain/lose*) to Connor that you thought would motivate him, the special treat if he stayed in bed.

3. You **connected** with him face to face before you spoke. You knew he was paying attention and heard you.

4. You **communicated** with him ONE time.

5. You **clarified** your instructions by role-playing Superman and being stuck like glue to the sheets. You also had Connor repeat back the instructions.

"Houston, we have lift-off!"

You correct when Connor gets out of bed one time. Why? Because you mean what you say when you say it, and because you CARE!

At this point in the book, we realize that you could be coming from any number of places when it comes to correcting a child. I (*Janis*) shared with you earlier about initially starting off as a lenient parent with my first-born son, Ryan. I believe that was a direct result of my harsh upbringing. As a child, I was punished but never corrected. And the punishment I received did *not* make any investment in my character bank. Yes, I was fearful of my parents, but in the end I was morally bankrupt.

I am so very thankful for the intervention of Jack and Cynthia Heald who mentored us in Tucson, AZ. They were my first loving and firm parental role-models. They coached us in being the parents Ryan needed us to be (the fence around his life) for his sense of security.

One of the first things they asked us to do was to watch for the next time Ryan said, *"No,"* to us. To this day, I can remember exactly when and where Ryan did this!

Ryan had refused to get dressed after his bath and was running away from my husband. I remember Dave and I looking at each other and saying, *"This is it."* I immediately got on the phone to Cynthia, while watching Dave correct Ryan for the first time. Cynthia had to keep reassuring me that we were doing the loving thing. She kept me focused on the possible *ripple effect* if we let this undesirable behavior go.

And then, right before my eyes, I saw my son transform. His tantrums turned into soft crying and he dissolved in my husband's arms. I could hear Ryan say, *"Can I put my clothes on now, Daddy?"*

It worked! I watched my husband correct as a loving and firm parent and my child respond to that correction with a tender heart. The contrast between the way I was punished as a child, to the way my husband corrected Ryan, was huge. There is a big difference between punishment and correction. (By the way, we use the word correct vs. discipline because we believe it communicates on the character level.)

Punishment vs. Correction

Punishment penalizes the child for their past misdeeds. It creates frustration and hostility on the part of the parent and fear and guilt on the part of the child.

The purpose of correction is to establish the desirable character and behavior. Correction is motivated by love and concern for the child, and promotes a feeling of security, like the fence on the playground.

	Punishment	Correction
Focus	To inflict penalty for an offence.	To establish positive character & behavior.
Parent's Feelings	Anger Hostility Frustration	Love Care Commitment
Child's Feelings	Fear Valueless Withdrawal	Security Valued Maturity

We are going to share with you a caring model for giving correction. But first, some thoughts:

❖ Again, the magic age of 15 months is when most experts agree you can begin correction. However, you know your child better than anyone else. Be sensitive as to when you should start. One of the indicators could be when your child reaches for something that is off limits, and pauses to look back at you. They are probably ready to be corrected as they are demonstrating, by their response, they are aware of their actions.

❖ Remember, for the very small child, praise and distraction may be enough to establish the desired behavior.

❖ Be diligent in your home to minimize and preferably avoid correcting in public.

❖ ALWAYS use the least amount of correction to extinguish the undesirable character or behavior.

Correct With CARE ♥

Confront

Act

Resolve

Evaluate

Confront

Confront simply means to be face to face and that you mean business.

❖ **Pick a neutral location.**
You are meeting one on one to avoid any embarrassment or to save face, on the part of the child. (The desire to not lose face in front of their peers or siblings can cause a child to resist correction). Again, you may want to give good instructions for where and how to go to the neutral location before there needs to be correction. Also, instruct them in what they will *gain/lose* to motivate them to walk quietly and quickly to the designated spot. This would be a good thing to role-play. The child should know, whatever they are doing, whomever they are with, when they hear you say, "*Meet me in the* _____ ," they do not pass go! They do not collect $200.

Going to a neutral location gives you both a breather. This provides you a few minutes to calm down in order to reflect and consider a course of action. *Take as much time as you need for decompression.* The child will also have a little time to soften his or her heart (or not).

You can think of what room would work well in your household. My *(Janis)* husband liked the bathroom because he had a place to sit down!

If Connor gets out of bed one time, you say, *"Connor, meet me in the laundry room."*

❖ **Appeal to their conscience.**
The first words out of your mouth when you are face to face in your neutral location is, *"What did you do?"* This question directly appeals to the conscience and character of the child. Conscience is the moral judgment distinguishing between right and wrong. Because you want to engage the conscience and invest in the character of your child, attempt to avoid manipulative statements that could create an

emotional, argumentative or volatile response.

The statements below could be manipulative on the part of the parent. They appeal to something other than the child's conscience and therefore, does not invest in the child's character bank.

Pick the motive the parent may be engaging in with each sentence:

"Connor, you will have to be punished for what you did!"
- o Intellect
- o Will
- o Physical *(We'll give you a hint...it's this one.)*
- o Emotional

"Connor, you hurt me when you did that."
- o Intellect
- o Will
- o Physical
- o Emotional

"Connor, promise me that you will never do that again."
- o Intellect
- o Will
- o Physical
- o Emotional

"Connor, do you think that was the smart thing to do?"
- o Intellect
- o Will
- o Physical
- o Emotional

If you appeal to their *physical*, they can react and see you as unjust.

If you appeal to their *emotions*, they can appease you but it will only be temporary.

If you appeal to their *will*, they can rebel and clam up.

If you appeal to their *intellect*, they can argue their point and become defensive.

BUT if you appeal to their *conscience*, "*Connor, what did you do?*", they can grow in character by humbling themselves and being honest *(super six)*.

Our *desire* is to have the child own the behavior and not justify or blame others. This can bring about permanent change. Ultimately, you want your child to do the right thing for the right reason. Granted that takes time and maturity, but it all starts now!

❖ **Communicate love and commitment.**
"I love you and that love wants the best for you."

You can use your own words, of course, to express yourself here, but it's important to communicate your level of commitment. Your child will know your love is relentless.

"Connor, meet me in the laundry room. What did you do? You got out of bed. I love you Connor and that love wants the best for you. Sleeping and being safe in bed is best."

Act

You have three options in carrying out correction for your child: *verbal, creative* and *physical*. Remember to always use the least amount of correction to change the character or behavior of your child.

1. Verbal

A firm *verbal* correction may be all you need to change the behavior or attitude of a child. How will you know if it was effective? The behavior is NOT repeated. However, the verbal correction is not done flippantly. You are still using the *entire* CARE*ing* model (you will have the complete picture by the end of the chapter).

Communicating your love and giving a verbal reprimand may be all that is needed to deter the undesirable behavior of a sensitive child. You could also share that you will up the ante *(gain/lose)*, with a repeated offense. You may not have it all figured out at the time, but you want the child to know that it will definitely be more severe. Hopefully, just the thought of going back in the laundry room will deter the behavior and you will never have to figure it out!

2. Creative

Creative correction means you are attempting to relate the correction to the offense. For example, if your child is hitting others you might say, *"Keep your hands to yourself, or I will give you a chore in the house where you can use your hands to help and not hurt."*

The creative correction could be a reward. *"I want you to do what is right and be kind to others. I am going to put four quarters in your jar. If you keep your hands to yourself today, I will give you another quarter to put in your bank. But for every time you use your hands to hurt, you will give me a quarter. At the end of the week, let's see how many quarters you have and we can go shopping as a reward!"*

If this is effective, the creative correction can be tapered off once the desired behavior becomes the norm. Keep the creative correction simple, however, because you will need to follow through with *whatever* you set up. We do not want to add stress to your day with a complicated system. As an alternative, consider using "screen time." This could help two-fold, it controls the amount of time the child is connected to technology, and is extremely motivating so you won't have to work so hard.

Consider involving your child in the process. *"I need to correct this behavior/attitude. What correction do you think we should use? You can pick it this time, but if you do it again I will pick it"* (*gain/lose*). You will be surprised to see how much harder they are on themselves. Use your creative genius, and if you are found wanting, network with other committed parents.

In our scenario with Connor in the Instruct chapter, we used creative correction with what he could *gain/lose,* his special snack he picked. If he gets out of bed you will do the complete CARE*ing* model of correction:

"Connor, what did you do? You got out of bed. I love you Connor and that love wants the best for you. Sleeping and being safe in bed is best."

After you speak with him, you immediately walk him to the counter to put the snack back in the drawer. He lost that by disobeying you. That was not a great loss, obviously, since he got up, so you will need to up the ante.

Before Connor goes back to bed, tell him what he will *gain/lose* if he gets up the next time. You could up the ante and use his favorite stuffed animal he sleeps with. (*I know this may be harder for you than him.*) He stays in bed, he keeps the stuffed animal; he gets out of bed, he loses his stuffed animal. When Connor thinks the loss is too great to pay, he will stay in bed.

You as a parent have to know your child and find what is going to motivate them. And, the quicker the better! However, having your child grasp the truth that you will indeed do *everything* you say may be enough to establish the desirable behavior!

"Time-Out"

A creative correction that parents often use is "time-out." We are not advocates of this because our desire is to have the correction be immediate and over! Time-out and grounding separates you emotionally and physically from your child or teen. Dragging the correction out with, "*Go to your room!*" may actually add to your stress. More importantly, the child may not be developmentally able to process alone what you had intended and is simply left to play and forget.

On the surface it may appear like a quick remedy, but with little cost to the child, the undesirable character or behavior is often repeated. In the long run, this wears you down as a parent. More importantly, very little is accomplished in the area of resolving conflict or investing in the character of the child. Lastly, omitting the correction of time-out, grounding, etc. minimizes the chance of your child/teen harboring any animosity against you. You are seen as a fair and just parent.

It is our *desire* that we maintain a right relationship, as best we can, with our children as they grow into adulthood.

Having said all that, if and when you do use time-out, make sure it is in your sight, brief and you follow the entire CARE*ing* model.

3. Physical

Physical correction is still legal in every state. When you do up the ante this could be a possibility. We do want you to be aware of what your current state law allows, especially if you have your child in a public institution. For example, we live in WA State and searched under *correcting a child* and found our WA policy:

1. *RCW 9A.16.100 Use of force on children-Policy-Actions presumed unreasonable.*

2. *It is the policy of this state to protect children from assault and abuse and to encourage parents, teachers, and their authorized agents to use methods of correction and restraint of children that are not dangerous to the children. However, the physical discipline of a child is not unlawful when it is reasonable and moderate and is inflicted by a parent, teacher, or guardian for purposes of restraining or correcting the child. Any use of force on a child by any other person is unlawful unless it is reasonable and moderate and is authorized in advance by the child's parent or guardian for purposes of restraining or correcting the child. The following actions are presumed unreasonable when used to correct or restrain a child: (1) Throwing, kicking, burning, or cutting a child; (2) striking a child with a closed fist; (3) shaking a child under age three; (4) interfering with a*

child's breathing; (5) threatening a child with a deadly weapon; or (6) doing any other act that is likely to cause and which does cause bodily harm greater than transient pain or minor temporary marks.

3. *The age, size, and condition of the child and the location of the injury shall be considered when determining whether the bodily harm is reasonable or moderate. This list is illustrative of unreasonable actions and is not intended to be exclusive.*

We are not lawyers, but to us this law is well balanced. It recognizes the need for parents to correct while protecting children from abuse.

It is interesting to see the results where physical correction has been out-lawed. Thirty years ago Sweden became the first country to impose a complete ban on physical discipline. Jason M. Fuller, of the University of Akron Law School of Sweden, saw it as the first and ideal laboratory to study the effects of spanking bans.

Here are the results of his study:

❖ Child abuse rates exploded over 500 percent according to police reports. *"Not only were Swedish parents resorting to pushing, grabbing and shoving more than U.S. parents, but they were also beating their children twice as often." Fuller*

❖ Fuller's analysis revealed after a decade of the ban, continual rates of abuse rose three times the U.S. rate and children under the age of seven endured an almost six-fold increase.

❖ *"Swedish teen violence skyrocketed in the early 1990s, when children, that had grown up entirely under the spanking ban, first became teenagers." Fuller noted. "Preadolescents and teenagers under fifteen started becoming even more violent toward their peers. By 1994, the number of youth criminal assaults had increased by six times the 1984 rate."*

Be assured, in the United States, we can still use physical correction as one of the CARE*ing* options. Below are some recent rulings here in the states.

❖ The New York State Appellate Division found that a Long Island father's spanking of an 8-year-old boy, *"was a reasonable use of force."*

"The father's open-handed spanking of the child as a form of discipline, after he heard the child curse at an adult, was a reasonable use of force and, under the circumstances presented here, did not constitute excessive corporal punishment," the four-judge panel ruled in an unanimous decision.

❖ A federal appeals court in California ruled last year that a woman who hit her 12-year-old daughter, in the rear with a wooden spoon, should not be labeled a child abuser.

❖ Courts in other states have also backed up parents who spanked their kids.

Read more: http://www.nydailynews.com/new-york/court-parents-spank-kids-article-1.1874088#ixzz39ODZ5cYe

71

When choosing this option, consider these things:

Take time to decompress and never correct out of anger.

Use a neutral object rather than your hand. You could simply place a wooden spoon on the counter to remind your child that you are watching. You may never have to use it. Just the fact that you laid it out and that you mean what you say when you say it, may be enough to distinguish the undesirable behavior.

Remember to use the least amount of correction to change the behavior.

Be diligent in your home to minimize and preferably avoid correcting in public. (*We know we said some of these things before, but they stand to be repeated.*)

Maintain an open communication with those in authority over your children.

Be aware of the changing culture and continue to stay as informed as possible.

"Do keep in mind that someone with good intentions may have differing opinions on what classifies as abuse and are mandated to report any concerns."
Ali Hanson, Elementary Teacher, MA in Teaching

Resolve

Though we cannot see into the heart of a child, there are signs that allow us to take a small peek. Resolution, or having the matter settled, can sometimes be seen within a child's tender heart. You can help to develop a tender heart in your child in three different areas.

Tender heart towards the:

1. **Correction**
   You are looking for signs that the child is sincerely sorry. Some signs that would indicate a change of heart could be body language, verbal communication or quietly crying. You may need to instruct your child initially that this is *always* the expected outcome when being corrected. There is no tolerance for screaming, kicking or tantrums (from the child).

2. **Parent**
   You should be able to touch, hug or kiss your child at any time during or after correction. If your child withdraws from your loving touch with contempt, then you know that your child still has a hardened heart towards you. And if so, you start the instruction process all over again reminding them of the desirable behavior. (*We hope you are not getting overwhelmed!*)

3. **Offended**
   If there is an offended party, for instance, your child pinches someone, your child must go back to resolve it and make it right. This happens *always* and *immediately* following correction.

Instruct your child to speak kindly, make eye-contact with the offended party and say the following:

"I am sorry for _____. Do you forgive me?"

Only the very courageous and committed parents go here, to reconciliation. We seldom see this done, but it is necessary for a couple of reasons:

It's important for your child to strive to maintain a clear conscience with others. *Ka-ching!*

Second, it can help to resolve conflict with the offended party.

Of course it would be nice if a sincere apology was always well received, but that can only be a *desire*. It's important to note that feelings are neither right nor wrong, they are just there. You cannot control feelings, but you can hold your child responsible for their actions.

Your own children should be instructed on how to receive an apology and come to a resolution. This instruction will help your family avoid building up those blocks we talked about in the Invest chapter. Instruct the offended child to say these words:

"Yes, I forgive you for _____."

Remember, if either child is unwilling to make it right as instructed, it's back to the laundry room (*gain/lose*)!

In our example, Connor was dishonest with you by getting out of bed. You, the parent, are the offended party. Before you leave the laundry room, you want Connor to say, *"Do you forgive me for getting out of bed?"*

It is immediately resolved and there is no animosity between the parent and child. As Connor grows into a teen, adult, husband and father, he will be able to draw from the values of respect, integrity, humility and forgiveness that you invested in his character bank early on. As a loving and firm parent, you are making a huge impact in shaping this boy into the man you *desire* him to be.

Evaluate

It's not over quite yet. Quickly process how the correction went by asking yourself some questions:

❖ How did the correction go?

❖ Did my child have a soft heart towards me?

❖ Did my child make it right?

❖ Did I overcorrect? (If so, go and make it right immediately with your child.)

This CARE*ing* model for correction may seem tedious and difficult for you to implement at first. Parents, you may want to warn your children, spouse, grandparents and neighborhood: *"I am changing."*

As soon as your child understands your level of commitment, you will begin to see results. Your child will most likely stop the undesirable behavior because your love is persistent and because they dread the laundry room. ☺

But more importantly, you are no longer spent as a parent! Keep your focus on the prize. The prize being the dividends you will enjoy from making this investment. Remember those from the first chapter? (*You might want to read those again!*)

 Bring it Home

❖ Agree on your neutral location for correction.
❖ Begin practicing the CARE*ing* model, as needed:
   Confront
   Act
   Resolve
   Evaluate
❖ What will you use to correct the issue that is driving you crazy? (*Verbal, Creative, Physical*)

Remember, good instruction helps eliminate the need for correction.

Chapter 7

FINISH

"It takes courage to invest the excess in others
when you could be indulging yourself. It takes courage to say
no to wants that would only complicate your life. Loving
takes time and time requires sacrifice...somewhere.
Effective parenting cannot be done by accident.
We have to parent on purpose."
Tim Kimmel, Little House on the Freeway

Do you remember the objective in our writing
REALSIMPLE**PARENTING**? We wanted *you* not to be
put out as a parent. Our *desire* is that you are experiencing
more joy in parenting, as you consistently use the three
simple steps, **Instruct**, **Reflect** and **Correct**.

I (*Janis*) loved my role as a mother! The investment I made
in the little ones entrusted to me helped them grow into the
adults they are today. I loved helping to shape the small
child and even enjoyed the teen years. I miss it all! I can
remember it like it was yesterday, Dave and I sitting in lawn
chairs watching the five children play together. I wanted to
freeze time right then. I didn't want it to end because I knew
what I was doing, parenting the five children, was
paramount.

In the beginning of the book we said we would share the
positive *ripple effect* we experienced with RSP. We could not
have known, when we started as loving and firm parents
committed to the character of our children, the far-reaching
dividends.

❖ Right away, when we began investing in our children's
character bank, we saw change! Our first born children
realized at an early age that the three simple steps, instruct,
reflect, and correct, were the new norm. It even helped in
our marriages because we were on the same page in regards

to parenting. And because we were not spent in the area of parenting, we had more time and energy to serve outside our home in our schools, communities and careers.

❖ Each sibling imitated the desired character and behavior of the first-born. That made our job of parenting soooo much easier!

❖ The children were respectful of one another, resolving their own conflict, which brought harmony and peace to our home.

❖ It continued on with the children being and choosing wise friends and being secure in who they are. They were leaders and role-models in their schools.

❖ As adults they made a difference as they began serving in their community and country.

❖ It continued in their work place as we saw them serve with integrity and a spirit of excellence in their chosen fields.

❖ We continue to see it in their marriage relationships as they are responsible, committed and quick to resolve conflict as a spouse.

❖ And finally, we watch them raise our beloved grandchildren with the same investments.

Can you see what a big difference these three little steps can make? It's the gift to yourself that keeps on giving, for generations to come.

In closing, let us share one last thing with you. Kay Coles James wrote an article called, *That Delicate Balance.* She was the Secretary of Health and Human Resources for the commonwealth of Virginia in 1994. She went from the poverty of her past to the corridors of the White House.

She said this, *"Although the life with which God has blessed me is wonderful, it is often difficult, and sometimes I become weary to the point of tears. Most of all, I struggle to fulfill my commitment to my family."*

She went on to share that she often feels like an imperfect juggler with too many balls in the air. She refers to the balls as either rubber or crystal. Rubber balls, like civic obligations, volunteer work, and social life, she can occasionally let go of. If they fall to the floor they would bounce. Crystal balls, like her faith, and being a wife and a mother, if allowed to drop could shatter.

We are asking you to consider letting go of those balls that are rubber in your life in order to keep the crystal one of parenting from shattering. Your children are crystal!

I (*Susan*) can remember being offered what I thought was my dream job. It was an opportunity of a lifetime. I was parenting my three school-age kids and could have certainly used the additional income, as well as advance in my career. But I chose to invest in my children and stayed with my current job that allowed me to do that. The dividends came years later when we would hear from our adult children's professors, Army officers and employers that we had done something right. I cannot think of anything else I would have rather invested my time and energy in!

We are not writing this because we were perfect parents who produced perfect children. We certainly had our share of conflict and turmoil over the years, but we know it was minimized with our diligence in parenting. We want to encourage you to make it a *goal* to maintain that delicate balance as you juggle the commitments in your life. Actually, the fact that you've come to the end of our book is a good indicator that you are keeping the crystal ball of parenting your children from shattering. Thank you!

Bring it Home

After reading and applying **REAL**SIMPLE**PARENTING,** the character or behavior that was driving you crazy in the beginning of the book should be wrapped up by now. Please let us know what's working and what's not. Consider us another sounding board for you. Send us any parenting ideas, and if we think they could help other parents, we will post them, with your permission, on our website: www.realsimpleparenting.com

 Stay connected with us on Real Simple Parenting Facebook page.

And please think of another parent you could help by giving them our book. Thank you again for letting us come along side of you!

Three Simple Steps in a Nutshell

1. Instruct
* ❖ **Choose** to be sensitive to battles, age, fatigue.
* ❖ **Calculate** what the child will *gain/lose.*
* ❖ **Connect** at eye-level, making eye contact.
* ❖ **Communicate** kind but firm, positive and brief.
* ❖ **Clarify** by role-modeling and child repeats back.

2. Reflect
* ❖ Am I certain?
* ❖ Am I capable?
* ❖ Am I consistent?

3. Correct
* ❖ Confront: *"What did you do?"*
* ❖ Act: Verbal, Creative, Physical/ Least amount.
* ❖ Resolve: Look for a tender heart.
* ❖ Evaluate: How did that go?

ABOUT THE AUTHORS

Janis and Susan have been faithful friends for over 25 years. They met in Phoenix, AZ as young mothers. With the help of their devoted husbands, they were committed to raising their children to be men and women of character. Over the years, they have grown and served in a variety of areas, both single and together. Now, with their combined expertise, wisdom, and resources they make a dynamic team in the area of parenting.

You can learn more about them and book a speaking engagement for your group or organization on their website: www.realsimpleparenting.com

Index

Making your life easier!

Made in the USA
San Bernardino, CA
13 May 2016